Darkest Hours

Alden R. Carter

★ DARKEST HOURS ★

DISCARD

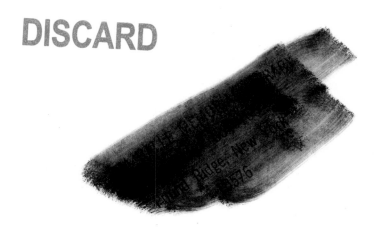

Franklin Watts
New York/London/Toronto
Sydney/1988
A First Book

Library of Congress Cataloging-in-Publication Data

Carter, Alden R.
Darkest hours / Alden R. Carter.
p. cm.—(A First book)
Bibliography: p.
Includes index.
Summary: Describes events and battles during the early years of
the Revolutionary War, including campaigns at Lexington and Concord,
Bunker Hill, Trenton, and activities at the Continental Congress.
ISBN 0-531-10578-4
1. United States—History—Revolution, 1775–1783—Campaigns
Juvenile literature. [1. United States—History—Revolution,
1775-1783—Campaigns.] I. Title. II. Series.
E231.C33   1988
973.3'31—dc19

88-5620   CIP   AC

For my friend and editor,
Marjory Kline

Other Books by Alden R. Carter

Contents

Many thanks to all who helped with *Darkest Hours,* particularly my mother, Hilda Carter Fletcher; and my friends Don Beyer, Dean Markwardt, Sue Babcock, and Georgette Frazer. As always, my wife, Carol, deserves much of the credit.

★ 1 ★

Call to Arms

The drum of approaching hoofbeats reached Colonel Israel Putnam as he heaved another stone onto the half-finished wall. He slapped dust from his leather apron and turned to gaze up the road to the north. Putnam was a short, powerful man, the strength of his frame and the fire of his spirit unweakened by his fifty-seven years. His pulse quickened as the hard-riding messenger came into view. For months, Putnam had daily expected news of war. Had it finally happened? Would there be action at last?

The hired men watched their employer's scarred face. "Old Put" was a folk hero in Connecticut. On winter evenings, children listened breathlessly to tales of his adventures. He had been captured in a frontier battle during the French and Indian War in the 1750s. The Indians had tied him to a stake, then danced as he stood defiantly with flames crackling around his feet. Only a last-second rescue by a French officer had saved him. Other stories told of Putnam's long captivity in Montreal; of shipwreck on the wild coast of Cuba; and of how, one terrible winter night, he had fought and killed a werewolf. With the exception of the last, most of the stories contained a surprising amount of truth: the Connecticut farmer was indeed a man to be reckoned with.

The rider brought his sweating horse to a hard stop before Putnam and thrust a much-handled letter at him. Putnam scanned the hastily written lines. At break of day on April 19, 1775, British troops from Boston had fired on colonial militiamen at Lexington and soaked the village green with patriots' blood. Putnam roared for his horse and musket.

New England in Rebellion

As Putnam rode north, he found the country lanes already filled with militia companies on the march. Wild and contradictory rumors swept their ranks, but Putnam gradually pieced together a picture of the terrible events of the previous day. British troops had marched on Lexington to capture the patriot leaders John Hancock and Samuel Adams. Two messengers from Boston, Paul Revere and William Dawes, had spread the alarm to the countryside in time for Hancock and Adams to escape. The badly outnumbered Lexington militia had defied the British and had been ruthlessly shot down.

The British had marched on to seize the military supplies stored at Concord. Again they were too late, and again there was fighting. The British began their 15-mile return march to Boston through an enraged countryside. By the afternoon, thousands of colonists were firing on the British column from the cover of stone walls, trees, barns, and houses. The British struck back, and scores died on both sides. The British had finally escaped, but the colonists surrounded Boston, swearing revenge.

Putnam regretted missing the battle, but he was not a man who dwelt much on the past or thought very far into the future. It was enough to know that America had finally rebelled against the tyranny of the British king and government—and that Israel Putnam would soon be in the thick of the fight for liberty.

The News Spreads South

Dispatch riders carried the news of Lexington and Concord south from New England. Horses died of exhaustion, riders fainted with fatigue, but the news kept moving. New York got it on April 23. The next day, it arrived in Philadelphia, the largest and richest of America's cities. By the second week in May, it had reached Savannah, Georgia, the southernmost city in the thirteen colonies.

Most Americans were shocked and outraged by the news. Throughout the colonies, militia companies began drilling as local committees hurriedly gathered arms and supplies. Yet far from *all* Americans favored a war for independence. Despite more than a decade of British misgovernment, many colonists still felt a deep loyalty to the king and the institutions of the British Empire. Some would decide to stand with their patriot neighbors. Others would call themselves Loyalists and fight for the king

The news of Lexington and Concord had reached Philadelphia as delegates from the colonies were gathering for the second meeting of the Continental Congress. The Congress had first met in the fall of 1774 to discuss a united stand against the unfair taxes and laws laid on America by Parliament, Britain's national assembly.

The outbreak of fighting forced huge new responsibilities on the delegates. Few of them had wanted war, but now—like

*Dispatch riders carried the news of
Lexington and Concord south from New
England, calling the colonists to arms.*

it or not—they had a revolution on their hands. Congress lacked the authority or power to govern the thirteen colonies, yet no other body existed to speak for America. Congress had to either find a peaceful solution to the conflict between mother country and colonies—or prepare for a long and bloody war. Urgent calls went out for still-absent delegates to hurry to Philadelphia.

Boston under Siege

There could be little doubt that war had come to New England. Under the command of General Artemas Ward, Massachusetts' militia chief, troops from several colonies were laying siege to Boston. The militiamen dug trenches and built fortifications to cut the city off from the countryside. The most violent patriots called for an immediate attack on the British army in Boston; one quick and overwhelming victory, and America would be free.

Ward knew better than to attack. The British commander, General Thomas Gage, had some forty-five hundred highly trained soldiers in the city, powerful warships in the harbor, and reinforcements on the way. Fighting from behind the city's fortifications, the British could slaughter Ward's poorly trained militiamen.

Ward knew his army's weaknesses. His troops had no uniforms, few cannon, an ample number of muskets but little powder, and a distinctly unmilitary attitude. The men had little respect for authority and came and went as they pleased. What training they had amounted to an understanding of a few parade-ground commands. Worst of all, they had almost no experience. A few men had fought alongside the British in the war against the French and the Indians, but the vast majority were ignorant of the frightening realities of war. Their only advantage lay in numbers, and numbers would not be enough against Gage's battle-hardened troops.

Ward decided that the best chance for success lay in trying to starve the British out. He ordered the siege works extended until they covered a vast semicircle from Charlestown Peninsula to Boston Neck, the narrow strip of land separating Boston from the mainland. He gave orders for increased drills and did his best to see that the company commanders obeyed.

Inside Boston, General Gage had problems, too. Gage was a wise and careful soldier. He had repeatedly warned his superiors in London about the dangers of an expedition into the countryside, but they had insisted. At Lexington, a single—probably accidental—shot had triggered a war that Gage did not have the means to win. He could defend Boston, but his troops were far too few to regain control of Massachusetts, much less New England. He strengthened the city's defenses and waited for reinforcements. Deprived of fresh food from the countryside, his troops grumbled as they ate their rations of salt beef and dried beans. Their appetites would have been even less hearty had they known of events happening far to the west.

Ticonderoga

A tumbledown fort in northeastern New York held the means to end the siege of Boston: plenty of cannon. Fort Ticonderoga occupied one of the most strategic sites in North America. A few miles to its south lay Lake George, the route to the Hudson River Valley and the Middle Atlantic colonies. To the north stretched Lake Champlain, the ideal invasion route into Canada.

Preparing to attack the fort were two hugely ambitious men: Benedict Arnold and Ethan Allen. At thirty-four, Arnold was a man of many accomplishments. He was a superb athlete, a crack shot, an expert sailor, and a successful merchant. With a muscular, compact build and dark, handsome features, he charmed women and attracted the loyalty of men. A newly appointed militia colonel, he had great courage, but little patience and an arrogance that had already earned him a number of enemies. The events of the next few years would demonstrate his brilliance but reveal that he was dedicated to little but his own ambitions.

Ethan Allen was thirty-seven, a tall, lean, immensely strong backwoodsman. He was the colonel of the Green Mountain Boys, a militia unit that had been preserving New Hampshire's hold on present-day Vermont against the claims of New York. Allen had little formal education but had read widely. He had passion and courage, but often lacked good judgment. And, like Arnold, he was more interested in glory than the cause of liberty.

The two men were bitter rivals. Arnold demanded command of the expedition against Ticonderoga on the basis of his rank in the Massachusetts militia. Allen would have none of it; he had the loyalty of his Green Mountain Boys and the backing of several Connecticut patriots bankrolling the expedition. A compromise made Arnold and Allen joint commanders, but the real power belonged to Allen.

Fortunately, the taking of Ticonderoga presented little difficulty. The American force of about eighty-five men landed a half mile below the fort at daybreak on May 10, 1775. The frontiersmen poured through an unbarred gate, quickly made prisoners of the sentries inside, and rushed up a flight of stairs to the officers' quarters, where they were greeted by a sleepy lieutenant in his underwear. The British officer asked by what authority they trespassed on the king's property. Allen thundered—according to his account, at least—"In the name of the Great Jehovah and the Continental Congress!"

Soon roused, the fort's commander surveyed Allen's troops and decided their numbers carried adequate authority with or without the backing of God and the Congress. He surrendered his small garrison. Two days later, Allen's second-in-command, Seth Warner, captured the nearby fort at Crown Point without opposition.

Both Allen and Arnold viewed the capture of the forts as the beginning of a glorious campaign to take Canada. Neither wanted to share the glory with the other. Gathering a few troops, Arnold set out by boat to attack the fortified town of St. John's on the Richelieu River north of Lake Champlain. He plundered the town, then withdrew at the approach of a strong British relief force. On the way south, Arnold's force passed Allen's rowing north. Confronted by the British regulars, Allen soon reversed direction.

Congress Gets the News

The Continental Congress in Philadelphia received news of Arnold's and Allen's escapades with a mixture of joy and horror. The taking of Ticonderoga was a triumph, but an invasion of Canada might sour any hope for peace with Britain. Congress ordered a halt to expeditions north and dispatched Colonel Benjamin Hinman to take command at Fort Ticonderoga. Reduced to second-in-command, Arnold resigned in a huff.

Allen too was soon demoted. His men elected Seth Warner as their new colonel, in part because Allen had half-starved them by neglecting to bring any food along on their brief expedition into Canada. Allen departed to seek fame elsewhere. He was captured on a later invasion of Canada and spent years in a Montreal prison before he was exchanged for a British officer.

*Ethan Allen and his Green Mountain Boys capture
Fort Ticonderoga. Replying to the British
officer's query as to by what authority they
trespassed, Allen thundered, "In the name of the
Great Jehovah and the Continental Congress!"*

After that, he conspired with the British against the Continental Congress, then with the Congress against the British, and eventually threatened to "wage war with human nature at large." He died early enough to become a folk hero. History had much more in store for Benedict Arnold.

Congress Deliberates

Enough delegates had hurried to Philadelphia in time for Congress to open on May 10. Its members included a remarkable number of able and accomplished men. They would need all their wisdom to guide America through the troubles ahead.

Some delegates argued for an all-out war for independence. Others maintained that a reconciliation with Britain could be honorably negotiated. The delegates compromised by voting to pursue both options. Congress would ask the king once more for a guarantee of colonial rights. At the same time, Congress would begin organizing an army. In mid-June, Congress voted funds for a continental army and selected George Washington, the colonies' best-known soldier, as its commander in chief.

George Washington, gentleman farmer, hero of the French and Indian War, a tall and dignified man whose very bearing gave people confidence, had deep doubts about his abilities to lead the army to victory. He did not, however, doubt the honor and glory of the American cause. He waited impatiently while the Congress appointed his subordinate generals, then set off for Boston. The war did not wait for him to arrive.

Two days after Congress appointed Washington commander in chief, a savage battle interrupted the stalemate in Boston. The battle of Bunker Hill would teach the Americans and the British some bitter and bloody lessons.

★ 2 ★

—————— Pitched Battle ——————

General Artemas Ward had labored since spring to maintain the siege of Boston. His militiamen came and went, but by June he had a fairly stable force of some fifteen thousand camped around Boston. A few small skirmishes over livestock and hay were fought on the harbor islands, but otherwise little action broke the calm. British and American sentries traded gossip between the opposing fortifications on Boston Neck. Ward and General Gage agreed to an exchange of patriots from Boston for Loyalists from the countryside.

Late in May, Gage began receiving his reinforcements. With them came three major generals: William Howe, Henry Clinton, and John Burgoyne. Gage might well have preferred three regiments of infantry instead of three ambitious generals, but he politely listened to their advice. The generals feared that the rebels might place cannon on Dorchester Heights south of the city. A few long-range guns firing from the heights could drive the British warships from the harbor and force Gage to abandon Boston. Lacking cannon, the rebels had not occupied the heights yet, but they might soon, unless the British got there first. Gage accepted his generals' suggestion and scheduled an expedition to occupy the heights for June 18, 1775.

A Night March

An outline of the British plan soon reached Ward's headquarters in Cambridge, thanks to the patriots' spy network in the city. Ward's council of war recommended seizing both Dorchester Heights and the high ground on Charlestown Peninsula to the north of Boston. Ward had doubts but gave way to the urging of Israel Putnam—now a general—and the other "fire-eaters" on his staff. The council decided that the Americans would occupy Charlestown Peninsula first and Dorchester Heights later.

On the warm, still night of June 16, about a thousand militiamen, under the command of Colonel William Prescott, marched across the narrow neck of land connecting Charlestown Peninsula to the mainland. From the neck to the village of Charlestown at its tip, the peninsula measured about a mile, and at its widest point about half a mile. Three hills dominated the peninsula: 110-foot Bunker nearest the neck, 75-foot Breed's overlooking the village, and low Moulton's at the farthest corner of the peninsula.

After some debate among the officers, the men were put to work digging an earthen fortress called a redoubt on Breed's Hill. The work went fast—the militiamen-farmers may have been unfamiliar with many of the tools of war, but they were thoroughly acquainted with shovels and pickaxes. At first light, the lookout on the British warship *Lively* was horrified to see a rough redoubt, 130 feet on a side and 6 feet high, crowning

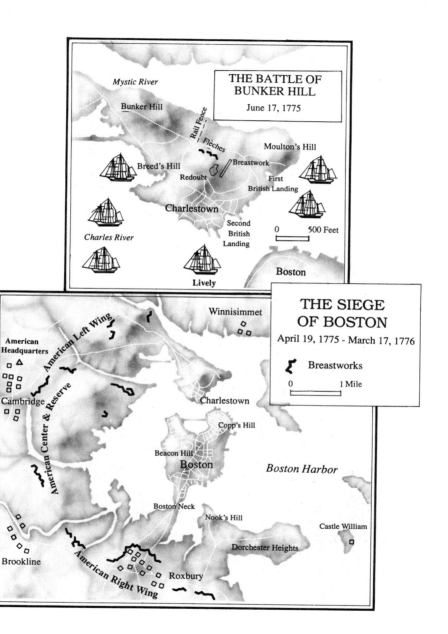

THE BATTLE OF
BUNKER HILL
June 17, 1775

Mystic River

Bunker Hill

Rail Fence

Fléches

Moulton's Hill

Breed's Hill

Breastwork

Redoubt

First
British
Landing

Charlestown

Second
British
Landing

Charles River

0   500 Feet

Boston

Lively

THE SIEGE
OF BOSTON
April 19, 1775 - March 17, 1776

Breastworks

0   1 Mile

Winnisimmet

American Left Wing

American Headquarters

American Center & Reserve

Cambridge

Charlestown

Copp's Hill

Beacon Hill

Boston

Boston Harbor

Boston Neck

Nook's Hill

Castle William

Brookline

Dorchester Heights

American Right Wing

Roxbury

Breed's Hill. Alerted, the ship's captain gave the order to fire. Other ships and a shore battery across the bay in Boston joined in a thunderous bombardment, eventually bringing some eighty guns to bear on the redoubt.

The cannon fire caused little damage to the walls—also called ramparts—of the redoubt, but it unnerved some of the militia. A few of the men drifted away, but when Colonel Prescott climbed a rampart and strolled casually along its rim in full view of the British gunners, most of the men kept digging. Beneath his calm exterior, Prescott was worried. He knew that his position could be flanked on the left by attackers staying out of musket range until they were in position to launch a charge from the rear. He ordered his men to dig a breastwork—a trench with an earth wall in front—from the redoubt down the slope of the hill to a small swamp, a distance of some 300 feet.

The day turned hot as the digging and cannonading continued. The patriots suffered from fatigue, thirst, and hunger, but they managed to finish the redoubt and breastwork by late morning.

The British Ready an Attack

Gage and his generals met in midmorning to debate their course of action. To avoid a house-to-house fight through Charlestown, Howe proposed landing troops below Moulton's Hill. He would then launch a flanking movement to encircle the redoubt—exactly the plan Prescott feared. Gage gave Howe permission to launch the attack.

Shortly after noon, fifteen hundred British troops, many of them crack grenadiers and light infantrymen, set out across the bay in a double line of twenty-eight barges. It must have been an awesome and terrifying sight for the tired militiamen watching from Breed's Hill. The scarlet-clad troops sat stiffly at attention. Row on row of bayonets glinted in the afternoon sun. On all sides, the cannon of the warships blazed. Clouds of powder smoke drifted across the scene, clearing to reveal the menacing barges a few oarstrokes closer. That all the Americans did not flee before the first barge reached shore is a wonder, explained only by Colonel Prescott's leadership and the patriots' strong belief in their cause.

The Lion's Pride

The British troops had every reason for confidence. They were the soldiers of the king, the best infantrymen in the world. They had won their reputation in countless battles against the best European armies. The coming fight with a few hundred farmers and villagers promised an easy victory.

The British army drew its enlisted men from the lowest levels of society. Criminals, vagrants, down-and-out workingmen, and naive country boys filled its ranks. Constant drilling and harsh discipline forged this rough material into a deadly weapon. Pay might be low, food poor, punishments severe, and the praise of civilians rare, but the army gave these men something they had never felt before: pride. A soldier's most precious possessions became his military skill and the reputation of his regiment.

The long hours of drill taught soldiers to obey scores of commands without hesitation. On the battlefield, companies and regiments maneuvered with clockwork precision. Rapid movements were made in column, three men abreast. To attack, the column faced left or right, and the soldiers advanced in ranks three deep. About fifty yards from the enemy, the ranks would halt, assume the firing position, and loose a volley from their Brown Bess muskets.

In the tight ranks, reloading took careful coordination. Officers gave eight separate orders to execute the procedure. (Colonial officers were forced to accept the individualism of their troops and gave only the single order, "prime and load.") Each soldier took a cartridge containing powder and ball from a pouch at his side. He tore off the end with his teeth and sprinkled some powder in the pan of the firing mechanism, where it would be ignited when the flint attached to the hammer struck the steel latch covering the pan. He then pushed the rest of the cartridge into the end of the barrel, drew a long steel ramrod from beneath it, rammed the charge home, and replaced the ramrod. Only then was he ready to "present and fire." A crack British company could fire about three volleys per minute.

The ten-pound Brown Bess was an inaccurate weapon with an effective range of less than one hundred yards. The inside of the barrel, or bore, was smooth and without the spiral grooves called rifling that gave sporting weapons greater range and accuracy by putting a spin on the bullet. Still, the Brown Bess could be fired faster than eighteenth-century rifles, and its .75-caliber ball, weighing more than an ounce, had tremendous stopping power.

After the volleys, the ranks would charge. With each step, men would fall dead or wounded, but the ranks would close and charge on to begin the real work. The military thinking of the day emphasized the use of the bayonet. Although a poor weapon for firing accurate shots, the Brown Bess served as an excellent handle for its twenty-one-inch bayonet. The British infantryman was at his most ferocious when "wielding the bay-onet" in the few minutes that decided most battles.

The British Officer

Officers with swords and pistols led the charge. Even generals often joined their men in the close fighting. Almost without exception, British officers were stupendously brave. The officers came from the upper classes of society. They were gentle-men, set apart by birth, wealth, and education from the enlisted men. Many well-to-do families bought ranks, or commissions, for their younger sons, who would receive no inheritance un-der British law. The purchase of commissions was an accepted practice and resulted in some men reaching high rank in their early twenties.

Because of the complexity of infantry tactics, the army needed many officers. A standard regiment of ten companies had 37 officers and 440 enlisted men—a high ratio in any age. Com-manding the regiment was a colonel with a staff of six officers. Each company of 44 enlisted men had a captain and two lieu-tenants. The most honored post for a young captain was com-mand of one of a regiment's two elite companies. The tallest and strongest men were chosen for the grenadier company, which was used for particularly difficult assaults and protection of one flank of the regiment. Small, agile, quick-thinking men made up the light infantry company used for scouting, rapid attacks, and protecting the regiment's other flank. Often, as on June 17, 1775, grenadier and light infantry companies were de-tached from their regular regiments and organized into elite regiments for a special mission.

The British army in America contained its fair share of incompetents, but on the average, the British officer was brave, reasonably intelligent, and intensely loyal to his men, his class, his country, and his king.

Below the company officers were the noncommissioned officers, tough sergeants and corporals who had earned their stripes by long and faithful service. To these veterans fell the responsibility of setting an example and maintaining much of the discipline in the barracks, on the parade ground, and in battle.

Artillery and Cavalry

Artillery companies fought alongside the infantry. In sieges, heavy guns firing 12-, 24-, and 36-pound balls came into action. In addition to the long-barreled cannon, the artillerymen employed short-barreled howitzers and stubby mortars. These long-range weapons usually fired exploding shells, hollow iron balls filled with gunpowder.

On open battlefields, light field guns softened up the enemy before an infantry attack. A six-pound field gun had a range of some 1,200 yards. A highly trained crew of fourteen could load a 6-pounder more than a dozen times a minute. Solid cannon-balls were used at long and medium range. At short range, the crew fired fearsome canisters filled with small balls called grapeshot. Yet even light field guns were difficult to handle in a rapidly moving battle. General Howe brought only a few to Charlestown Peninsula and those mostly for show.

Most British generals were infantrymen and put small value in cavalry. Although useful for scouting, raiding, and foraging (hunting for supplies), cavalry was expensive to maintain and often seemed in the way on battlefields. Cavalry played no part in the battle of Bunker Hill and only a small part in most other battles of the American Revolution.

The Landing

British troops began landing on Charlestown Peninsula at about one o'clock in the afternoon. The location of the landing confirmed Colonel Prescott's fears of a flanking movement. He had been begging for reinforcements and supplies since morning. On Bunker Hill, Israel Putnam pleaded with his men to go forward, but they refused because of the cannon fire from the ships. Prescott could wait no longer. He ordered Captain Thomas Knowlton and two hundred men to cover the open land between the breastwork and the Mystic River. Knowlton's men took position behind a rail fence, reinforcing it with stones and rails from other fences. Between the breastwork and the fence, they dug three small, V-shaped entrenchments called flèches.

Help from the rear finally arrived when two regiments of New Hampshire militia under colonels John Stark and James Reed joined Knowlton's men. Walking to the edge of the cliff at the far end of the fence, Stark was horrified to find a narrow strip of undefended beach lying nine feet below. Here a British column could advance unseen and unheard until it was behind the American lines. Stark sent his best men scrambling down the cliff. They threw up a stone wall and formed behind it in three ranks.

The British Attack

Howe seemed in no hurry to attack. He sent scouts forward, then waited while his reserve of seven hundred troops crossed the bay. When the scouts came under fire from a few militia-men in Charlestown, warships fired red-hot cannon balls into the village and set it ablaze—the first of many villages and towns that the war would reduce to ashes.

Around 2:00 P.M., Howe was finally ready to attack. His second-in-command, Brigadier General Robert Pigot, would make a feint—a light attack intended to draw attention from the main attack—against the redoubt. The main attack would fall on the fence and the wall on the beach. Once the rebels gave way, Howe would encircle and take the redoubt.

In the sweltering afternoon heat, the British infantry stepped out to the music of fife and drum. Each man carried a sixty-pound pack and forty pounds of other equipment. The advance became ragged as the soldiers labored over fences, around ponds, and through deep grass. Only the light infantry on the beach made rapid progress. They advanced with their bayonets at the ready, intending to smash through the Americans without firing a shot.

At the stone wall, Stark's men held their fire until the front ranks of the onrushing light infantry were only fifty yards away. The first volley leveled the lead company. Without hesitation, the following ranks leaped over the fallen bodies and charged on. Stark's second rank fired. The column reeled, then came on again. Stark's men fired again, then again. Even the best infantry in the world could not keep up an attack against such ferocious fire. The light infantry fell back, leaving ninety-six dead on the narrow beach.

Colonists watch the battle of Bunker Hill from the rooftops of Boston.

BOSTON

CHARLES TOWN

*An engraving from a drawing made at
the time of the attack on Bunker Hill
and the burning of Charlestown*

A few minutes later, the crack grenadiers slammed into the rail fence between the beach and the breastwork. The massed musket fire of the Americans cut them down in long scarlet rows. Every man on Howe's personal staff was killed or wounded. Finally, the exhausted grenadiers retreated.

All along the line the attack had failed. Howe re-formed his men and revised his plan. This time he would feint against the fence and hurl his strength against the redoubt and breastwork. Fifteen minutes after the first attack, Howe launched his second.

At the redoubt, Prescott gave his legendary order, "Don't fire until you see the whites of their eyes." At a hundred feet, the militia fired. The British fell by the score. For thirty minutes, the long red line writhed under the fire of the militia, then it fell back broken.

The Final Attack

The British infantrymen deserved their reputation. After the frightful losses in the first two attacks, they re-formed and, strengthened by four hundred fresh troops from Boston, attacked a third time. This time they found the soft spot in the American defenses between the rail fence and the breastwork. They overran the flèches, wheeled, and drove the Americans from the breastwork. At the redoubt, the British came under only light fire as the Americans ran short of gunpowder. The British stormed over the walls, bayonets poised. The Americans fought back with rifle butts and stones.

In a few minutes it was over. The Americans who could break free from the fight made a dash for Bunker Hill. The militia at the rail fence gave them covering fire, then retreated.

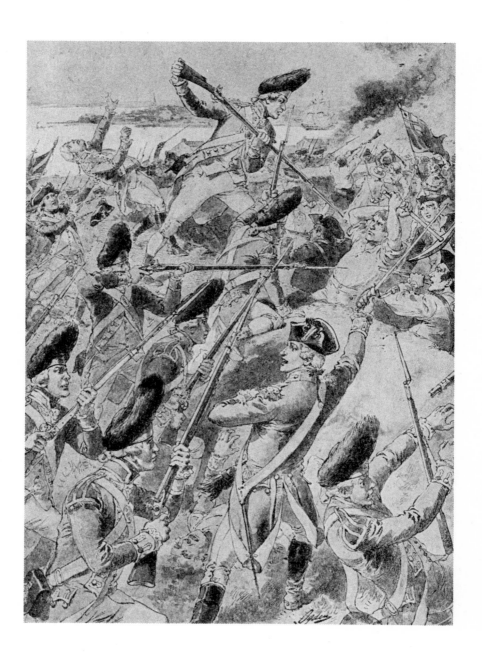

No attempt was made to hold Bunker Hill, and the Americans continued their flight across Charlestown Neck under the fire of the British warships.

The Reckoning

The British held the field, but at a terrible cost. Of the 2,400 British troops engaged, 1,054 including 92 officers had become casualties; 226 of them killed. Major John Pitcairn, the fine officer who had led the British troops in the fight at Lexington, died in the final assault on the redoubt. The American side counted 140 killed, 271 wounded, and 30 captured, most of the losses coming during the retreat. Among the dead was Dr. Joseph Warren, one of the most able of the patriot leaders.

In the aftermath of the battle of Bunker Hill—which should have gone down in history as the battle of Breed's Hill—both sides questioned whether Charlestown Peninsula had been worth fighting over at all. With so many fine troops dead and wounded, Gage was forced to cancel his attack on the more valuable Dorchester Heights. On the colonial side, General Putnam was criticized for strongly favoring the expedition, while General Ward was accused of timidity in failing to reinforce the defense in strength.

The battle had taught both sides some hard lessons. The British learned that the Americans—despite their ignorance of

In the final attack at Bunker Hill, British infantrymen overran the American defenses and drove the defenders from the redoubt.

the finer points of soldiering—could fight. In an open field, the militiamen probably would have fled, but behind earthworks and stone walls they would stand their ground. Any lingering belief that the patriots were only a cowardly mob lay dead on the battleground.

The Americans who had stood and fought could take pride in their accomplishment. Yet many in the rear had little to be proud of. The failure to send enough supplies—particularly water and the crucial gunpowder—was inexcusable. Reinforcements had stalled on the road for lack of direction. Perhaps a thousand militiamen—including many officers—had cowered on Bunker Hill rather than go forward. When the British had broken through the American lines and surrounded the redoubt on Breed's Hill, a determined counterattack from Bunker Hill or the fence line might have won the day. However, the Americans lacked the discipline, leadership, and even the bayonets for such an attack.

Numbers and patriotism did not make an army. If the patriots and their cause were to have any chance, the army needed a brilliant general capable of training and leading them to victory. Congress had chosen George Washington to fill that role. And he had doubts that it had chosen well.

A Gentleman Farmer Takes Command

Many of the militiamen eyed George Washington with suspicion when he rode into Cambridge on July 2, 1775. Who was this Virginia tobacco planter sent by the Continental Congress to take command of a New England army?

Even the most suspicious could not deny that Washington cut an impressive figure in his splendid blue uniform. He looked every inch the soldier whose deeds in the French and Indian War had been camp gossip for days. Boston's own John Adams—who was rapidly becoming one of the Revolution's most powerful leaders—had nominated Washington for commander in chief. On that recommendation alone, Washington deserved a chance to prove his ability.

Washington kept to himself the dismay he felt on first seeing the raw militia. He had made no secret of wanting to lead the Continental army. Now he had the job and, somehow, he would make these men into real soldiers.

Washington knew that politics had played a large role in his selection as commander in chief. Support for the Revolution

was uncertain in the South. Adams had nominated him in the hope that a southern-born commander in chief could rally other southerners to the cause of liberty. Yet, whatever the political reasons, Adams and Congress had chosen well—better than anyone, including Washington, could have known.

Washington had been born into a well-off planting family in 1732. As a young man, he had sought adventure as a surveyor on the Ohio frontier. During the French and Indian War, he won fame as a brave and skillful militia commander. In 1755, he served on the staff of General Edward Braddock during a disastrous expedition against Fort Duquesne, where Pittsburgh now stands. A French ambush killed Braddock and nearly destroyed the army, but Washington organized a skillful retreat. Yet Washington's courageous deeds had not won him a commission in the regular British army. Disappointed, he left military service in late 1758. He married and settled down to running the family's estates. In Virginia's assembly, the House of Burgesses, his quiet, reasoned opinions gained him respect. He was elected as a delegate to the First Continental Congress in the fall of 1774. He returned for the Second Continental Congress in the crisis following Lexington and Concord. He attended the spring session in his militia uniform, still hoping for peace but willing to fight.

At forty-three, Washington was a tall, muscular, handsome man with striking blue-gray eyes. On the surface, he maintained

The man chosen to lead the new Continental army was a forty-three-year-old Virginia tobacco planter named George Washington.

a calm, dignified—some said cold—manner. His words and actions were deliberate, and his very presence commanded respect. Beneath the surface, however, doubts often raged. Sometimes his responsibilities seemed overwhelming and the task ahead impossible. He had never commanded large forces, and his military training had been haphazard. Washington's doubts about his own ability and judgment occasionally made it difficult for him to reach quick and daring decisions. Yet too much confidence might have led to fatal errors in these early days of the war. Washington and his raw troops would learn from their mistakes.

Washington's most important qualities lay at the core of his being. He was a man of unbending integrity and courage. He believed with all his heart in what he called "the glorious cause" of defending America's liberties. And he believed that not only Congress but "Divine Providence" had chosen him to lead the fight. Whether the war would end for good or ill he did not know, but nothing would deter him from fighting it to the last ounce of his energy.

Reorganizing the Siege

Washington established his headquarters in Cambridge, some three miles from Boston, and set about strengthening the army's position. He ordered new and stronger siege works dug. He divided the approximately fourteen thousand troops into three divisions under major generals Artemas Ward, Israel Putnam, and Charles Lee. He ordered the generals to tighten discipline and drill their troops regularly.

Washington was a master of detail. He knew that even many of his senior officers understood few of the fine points of military life. He wrote countless detailed memos on such routine matters as latrine digging, food preparation, and general camp order. Few of the troops had uniforms, so Washington devised a system of colored ribbons and hat cockades to show rank.

Ward had done an excellent job of providing food and shelter for the troops, but the army lacked military supplies, particularly gunpowder. Washington sent messages to the New England colonies requesting supplies, but could not gather enough to make an attack possible. That was probably just as well, since the militia would have had little chance against the British defenses.

The summer wore on. Boredom and desertion took their toll in the spirits and numbers of the army. Yet, little by little, the army improved. A few skirmishes and bombardments took place. Some fourteen hundred Maryland, Virginia, and Pennsylvania frontiersmen, armed with long-range Kentucky rifles, joined the siege. An unruly lot, they disturbed discipline, but they were anxious to fight and Washington often sent them on raids. In October, he detached many of them for the biggest raid of all— an invasion of Canada.

Looking North

Early in the summer of 1775, Congress had reversed its earlier hesitancy to invade Canada. The former French provinces to the north were a threat. From Canada, the British could launch an invasion through Lake Champlain and down the Hudson River Valley to cut the colonies in two. Congress was also nervous about the recruiting efforts of the British among the Indians who had ravaged the frontier during the French and Indian wars.

Canada seemed an easy target. The best intelligence stated that the French Canadian inhabitants were likely to stay neutral.

An invasion force would face only seven hundred British troops under Canada's governor, General Sir Guy Carleton. In late June, Congress ordered General Philip Schuyler to organize an invasion force at Fort Ticonderoga.

Schuyler's expedition brought out the worst in the untrained colonial army. Schuyler, a wealthy New York landowner and a worthy patriot, lacked the military experience and temperament of a successful general. His troops were poorly equipped, lazy, and unruly. Regiments from different colonies refused to work together and frequently came close to blows. Much of the summer was lost in delay.

Schuyler's second-in-command, Brigadier General Richard Montgomery, a fine and experienced soldier, hated the waiting. Taking advantage of a brief absence of his superior, Montgomery finally got the expedition under way early in August. He laid siege to St. John's north of Lake Champlain. Schuyler joined him briefly before returning to Ticonderoga in poor health. Despite the insubordination and cowardice of many of his men, Montgomery finally took St. John's early in November. He moved on to Montreal and captured it on November 13, 1775, but the able General Carleton slipped away, dressed as a civilian. Carleton sailed down the St. Lawrence to Quebec, where another American force had emerged from the Maine forests to threaten the fortress city.

Arnold's March

While Schuyler and Montgomery were struggling to get their expedition going, Washington had formed a plan to invade Canada through Maine, a wilderness governed by Massachusetts. Benedict Arnold was hanging around the Cambridge headquarters without rank or duties. Washington offered him

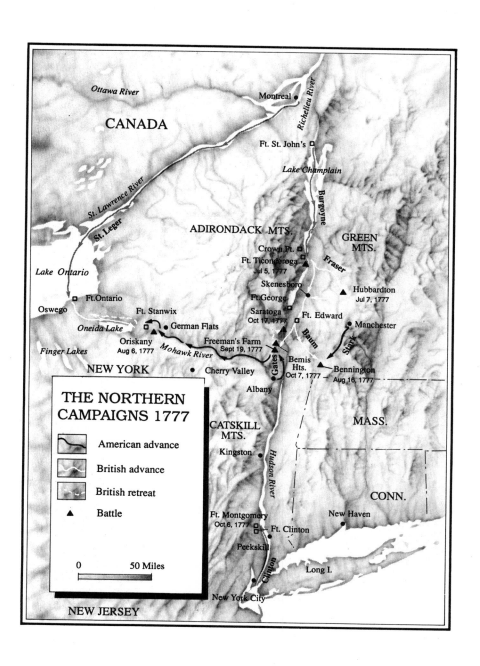

THE NORTHERN
CAMPAIGNS 1777

American advance

British advance

British retreat

▲ Battle

0   50 Miles

command of the expedition. Arnold jumped at the chance for glory.

For all his other abilities, Arnold had a shockingly poor sense of geography. He estimated that only 180 miles lay between Fort Western (today's Augusta, Maine) and the St. Lawrence River—a distance he planned to cover in twenty days. He organized an expedition of some eleven hundred men and set out from Cambridge on September 11, 1775.

The small army left Fort Western and civilization on September 24. Ahead of them lay not 180 but 350 miles of raging rivers, thick woods, and deep swamps. The weather turned cold. Constant rains drenched the men as they pushed flat-bottomed boats—called *bateaux*—northward against the current of the Kennebec River. Rapids smashed boats and ruined supplies. At waterfalls, the troops had to carry—or *portage*—the fleet of 400-pound bateaux and approximately 100 tons of supplies over fallen trees, up and down steep cliffs, and through knee-deep swamps.

By mid-October, almost all the boats had been destroyed, snow was falling, and food had all but given out. Some men turned back. Others dropped by the trail to die of hunger, fatigue, and disease. The rest of the army stumbled on, living on pine nuts, roasted shoe leather, and willpower. On November 9, after forty-five days on the march, an army of 675 scarecrows staggered from the woods to finally gaze upon the wide St. Lawrence. On the high bluff across the river lay Quebec, "the key to the continent."

Agony in the Snow

Arnold's men had made one of the great marches in military history, but their suffering would not earn them victory. Quebec had some two thousand hastily gathered defenders, stout

*Benedict Arnold's men trudging through the
Maine woods in a raging blizzard on their way
to attack Quebec in late December 1775*

walls, and 148 cannon. Arnold did not have the troops, cannon, or supplies for an attack. All he could do was place the town under siege and wait for reinforcements. Montgomery arrived from Montreal on December 2, with three hundred men and badly needed supplies. The two officers discussed the situation. A long siege was impossible: The enlistments of many of the men were due to expire with the year's end. Supplies for the remainder were scant. Quebec could easily hold out until spring, when the thaw would bring British reinforcements sailing up the river. The Americans had to attack despite the odds.

In a raging blizzard, they launched their doomed assault on the night of December 31, 1775. Montgomery and Arnold hoped to force a way through the lower town, then mount the bluff to the upper town and victory. But General Carleton had laid a trap in the narrow streets. In a savage fight, Montgomery was killed and Arnold severely wounded. Nearly half the American troops were killed or captured.

Arnold withdrew what was left of the army and camped a mile from the city. He received reinforcements on April 2, 1776. Arnold, his wound still unhealed, handed over command and retired to Montreal. A month later, a British attack routed the Americans and sent them scurrying west. The Americans made one more attempt to go on the offensive, attacking Trois-Rivières in June. They ran into a large, fresh British army under General John Burgoyne. Badly mauled, the colonial army retreated westward once again. By midsummer, Carleton and Burgoyne had chased all the remaining Americans from Canada. The colonies would never seriously threaten Canada again.

The Siege of Boston Goes On

Not all the American efforts of the winter of 1775–1776 ended in disaster. Washington continued to maintain the siege of Boston. The approach of winter weather added to his problems. His troops lacked fuel, winter clothing, and military supplies. Some of his aides suggested forming a small navy to capture British supply ships. To Washington's delight, the tiny navy of six schooners had immediate success. The British navy did surprisingly little to defend the merchant ships, other than to burn Falmouth (today's Portland, Maine) in an act of senseless revenge.

The capture of the ships added to the discomfort of the British cooped up in Boston. The siege had become so tight that almost all supplies had to be brought in by sea. British troops used wood from buildings, fences, and wharves for fuel. Smallpox and other diseases ravaged the underfed garrison. General William Howe, who had taken over command from Gage in the fall, saw little future in holding Boston. Even if he could break the siege, a campaign in hilly New England promised one bloody and indecisive battle after another. But Howe needed permission from far-off London and more ships to carry out an evacuation; he would have to spend the winter in Boston.

As 1775 drew to a close, Washington faced yet more problems. Most of the militiamen were nearing the end of their enlistments. The love of liberty that had brought them to Boston did not make them good or patient soldiers. They were tired, bored, and homesick. They had work to do on their farms or in their shops. Some militiamen responded to Washington's appeals to stay on, but thousands headed for home.

The task of recruiting and training a new army fell almost entirely on the commander in chief's shoulders. Ward was in poor health, Putnam hopeless when it came to administration, and the ambitious Lee an unreliable second-in-command. Despite the lack of support, Washington succeeded in repairing his army.

End of the Siege

While Washington labored, a twenty-five-year-old bookseller turned artilleryman was bringing him the tools to drive the British from Boston. Henry Knox was tall, wide, and thick—some 280 pounds thick. He was also skillful, efficient, and courageous—a true pillar of strength for Washington's army. In November 1775, Washington had sent him to Ticonderoga to inspect the fort's cannon. Knox selected forty-three guns, fourteen mortars, and a howitzer. He loaded them on ox-drawn sledges and started back across the roadless wilderness toward Boston. The march by Knox and his small force was a remarkable feat of endurance and skill. By late January, they were in Framingham, only miles from Boston. Washington sent congratulations and began preparations for an attack on the city.

Washington's generals advised against an attack. Instead, they urged him to occupy Dorchester Heights, where the cannon could be positioned to fire on the city and the British ships in the harbor. If Howe attacked, the Americans would slaughter the British regulars as they had in the early fighting in the battle of Bunker Hill. Washington agreed to the plan.

On the night of March 3, the Americans hurriedly fortified Dorchester Heights. Summoned by an alarmed aide at dawn, General Howe gazed south across the harbor and snapped, "The rebels have done more in one night than my whole army could do in months."

Howe considered attacking the heights, then thought better of it. He prepared to evacuate the city. Washington let the British load their ships in peace. There was an unspoken agreement between the two generals. If Washington kept his cannon silent, Howe would not burn Boston. On March 17, the British fleet set sail, carrying away eleven thousand troops and about one thousand Loyalists. British troops would never again return to Massachusetts.

★ 4 ★

"We Hold
These Truths..."

The British ships sailed north from Boston to Halifax, Nova Scotia, where the army could recover from the hardships of the long siege. Washington guessed that the British would next strike at New York City and prepared to move his army south. The pause in the war gave the colonies time to consider the events of the year since Lexington and Concord.

In Philadelphia, the members of the Continental Congress debated America's future. For months, Congress had been split between those wanting a reconciliation with Britain and those favoring a declaration of independence. As the spring of 1776 turned the land green, Congress edged toward a decision.

The Debate

Before the battle of Bunker Hill in June 1775, most delegates and the colonists they represented had favored reconciliation. Even the radicals led by Massachusetts's John Adams spoke of independence in cautious tones. News of the bloody battle caused the delegates to search their souls. With the death of so many, was reconciliation still possible? Yet was independence worth the terrible cost of war?

A month after the battle, Congress sent a letter, "the Olive Branch petition," to King George, asking him to find a peaceful solution to the conflict between mother country and colonies. As the petition made its slow way across the Atlantic, the British government was also debating the issues of peace or war. The prime minister, Lord Frederick North, was peaceable by nature, but he could not soothe others in the government or the angry king, who insisted that the colonies must obey the will of Britain or face the consequences.

Congress got news in October that the king had refused to receive their petition, declaring Congress illegal and its members traitors. He had ordered Lord North to prepare stern new measures to punish the colonies.

The Mounting Cost

The closing months of 1775 brought Congress news of more bloodshed. Reports dribbled into Philadelphia of battles in Canada and skirmishes around Boston. As troops from more colonies joined the fighting and the list of the dead lengthened, sentiment for independence grew.

Colonial assemblies were running the day-to-day business of government. The few royal governors who remained were ignored. Lord John Dunmore, Virginia's proud and bullheaded governor, enraged the southern colonies by calling for a slave uprising to defeat the rebels. Forced to flee to a Royal Navy warship, he ordered the shelling of Norfolk, Virginia, on the first day of 1776. The burning of the port added many southerners to the patriot ranks.

"Common Sense"

A pamphlet with the simple title "Common Sense" convinced countless thousands more of the wisdom and moral rightness of independence. Its author was a recent immigrant to America, Thomas Paine. Paine had been a poorly paid tax collector in England, only slightly better off than many of the poor he presented with tax bills. Poverty and unfairness outraged Paine. He set about trying to reform the system. He attempted to organize his fellow workers in a campaign for better wages, and was promptly fired. At the age of thirty-seven, he found himself a bankrupt failure in the eyes of society. He set sail for America late in 1774 with a handful of possessions, a letter of introduction from Benjamin Franklin, and hope for a brighter future.

The charged atmosphere of Philadelphia made Paine's spirits sing. Here in America lived a people who could "begin the world over again." He threw himself into the task of convincing Americans that they should become a free and independent people. He published "Common Sense" in January 1776, offering "simple facts, plain arguments, and common sense" to justify American independence: A continent should not be governed by a faraway island. British and American interests could *not* be reconciled. Kings and nobles were outdated; leaders should be chosen not by the circumstances of birth, but for character and talent.

With wit, shrewdness, and the occasional stirring phrase, Paine punctured the arguments for reconciliation. By the time Washington moved the army to New York City in April, 100,000 copies of "Common Sense" were circulating in the thirteen colonies. As popular opinion shifted, colonial assemblies began sending word to their delegates in Philadelphia that a vote for independence would receive approval at home.

A Question of Timing

News from Europe made passage of a declaration of independence almost inevitable. The British Parliament had published the Prohibitory Acts, outlawing all trade to and from the colonies. Any American ship captured on the high seas would become the property of the king. Even more shocking was the news that the British government was hiring thousands of German soldiers to help crush the revolt. For most delegates, the Prohibitory Acts and the hiring of mercenaries ended any hope of reconciliation. All that remained was to choose a time for a declaration of independence.

The debate in Congress over timing lasted into June 1776. The majority of the colonies were ready—Rhode Island had already declared itself independent—but a few still wavered. The delegates agreed that a united front was crucial to the success of the Revolution. Only a unanimous vote would tempt France and Britain's other European enemies into concluding alliances with America. Alliances would bring money, military supplies, and perhaps even troops and ships to aid the embattled colonies.

The Declaration of Independence

On June 11, Congress chose a committee to compose a declaration. The task of writing the first draft fell to the least busy of the five members, a young Virginia planter named Thomas Jefferson. At thirty-three, Jefferson was a striking man: tall, red-haired, handsome, charming, and rich. Yet what impressed such men as Franklin and John Adams was Jefferson's first-rate mind and wealth of knowledge.

In writing the Declaration of Independence, Jefferson called upon his wide reading in political philosophy to guide his own

The Declaration of Independence, one of the most important political documents in history, was drafted by a committee of five: Benjamin Franklin, Thomas Jefferson, John Adams, William Livingston, and Roger Sherman. Jefferson was its chief architect.

passionate belief in democracy. Adams and Franklin went over Jefferson's draft, toning down some of the phrasing that might offend a few wavering colonies. The committee presented the Declaration to Congress on July 2. After a few changes, the Congress approved the final draft on July 4, 1776. New York abstained at the last minute, but made passage unanimous eleven days later.

The Declaration of Independence was and remains one of the most important and moving political documents in history. Its most famous lines:

"We hold these truths to be self-evident, that all men are created equal, that they are endowed by their Creator with certain unalienable Rights, that among these are Life, Liberty and the pursuit of Happiness. —That to secure these rights, Governments are instituted among Men, deriving their just powers from the consent of the governed, —That whenever any Form of Government becomes destructive of these ends, it is the Right of the People to alter or to abolish it, and to institute new Government. . . ."

At the bottom of the document, the delegates signed beneath the words: "And for the support of this Declaration, with a firm reliance on the protection of divine Providence, we mutually pledge to each other our Lives, our Fortunes and our sacred Honor."

★ 5 ★

The Lion and the Fox

America had declared its independence to the world, but only victory on the battlefield could give the claim truth. A long and bloody task lay ahead.

In July 1776, the Americans faced the largest army Britain had ever dispatched from its shores. Five hundred ships landed an army of thirty-two thousand, including eight thousand German mercenaries, on Staten Island in New York Harbor. To oppose them, George Washington had an army of only nineteen thousand men, most of them poorly equipped and untested in battle. Against the twelve hundred guns of the British warships, he had only a few small batteries on Manhattan and Long Island. Nevertheless, he was determined to hold New York City. It was a decision that nearly led to the destruction of his army and the end of the Revolution.

Geography made the area an immense trap. New York City perched on a square mile at the tip of Manhattan, vulnerable to attack from either the Hudson River or the East River sides. Brooklyn Heights, across the East River on Long Island, domi-

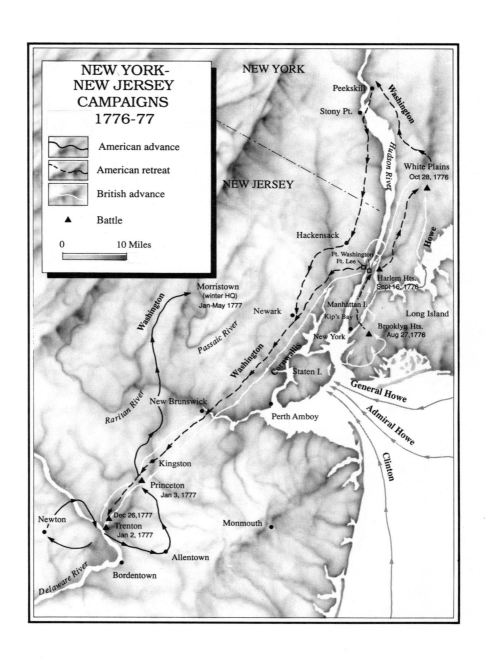

NEW YORK

Peekskill

Stony Pt.

Washington

Hudson River

NEW JERSEY

White Plains
Oct 28, 1776 ▲

Howe

Hackensack

Ft. Washington
Ft. Lee

Harlem Hts.
Sept 16, 1776 ▲

Morristown
(winter HQ)
Jan-May 1777

Washington

Newark

Manhattan I.

Kip's Bay

Long Island

Passaic River

New York

Brooklyn Hts.
Aug 27,1776 ▲

Washington

Washington

Cornwallis

Staten I.

General Howe

Raritan River

New Brunswick

Perth Amboy

Admiral Howe

Clinton

Kingston

Princeton
Jan 3, 1777

Newton

Dec 26,1777
Trenton
Jan 2, 1777

Monmouth

Allentown

Bordentown

Delaware River

nated the city much as Dorchester Heights dominated Boston. Washington would have to fortify both the city and Brooklyn Heights, but his feeble batteries could not prevent British warships from sailing up the East River to stand between the divided halves of his army. Control of the harbor and the rivers would give the British the power to strike almost anywhere they chose. The most deadly move would be to land infantry far to Washington's rear, where the Harlem River divided Manhattan from the mainland. By holding Kingsbridge, the only crossing, British troops could trap the Americans on Manhattan.

Washington should have recognized the impossibility of holding the city and withdrawn into the countryside, but the former militia colonel was still learning his trade. Later in the war, the British would call him the fox, but in the summer of 1776 Washington had yet to learn cunning.

The Battle of Long Island

One of Britain's finest generals commanded the huge army on Staten Island. At forty-six, Lieutenant General William Howe was a tall, rather broad man with a taste for high living. In nearly thirty years of military service, he had seen much blood spilled. He disliked wasting good troops for little gain, and the memory of Bunker Hill was much on his mind. In the new campaign, he intended to move carefully, preserving as much of his army as possible while he wore down Washington.

Howe decided to defeat the American army on Long Island before trying to trap the defenders of Manhattan. On August 22, he landed fifteen thousand British troops at Gravesend Bay on Long Island. Three days later, he added several thousand Germans—Hessians, as they were called by the Americans—to the already powerful force.

Between Gravesend Bay and the American positions on Brooklyn Heights lay a heavily wooded ridge called the Heights of Guan. Major General John Sullivan, a solid if unimaginative American officer, was in charge of guarding the four roads over the ridge. He had posted some twenty-eight hundred Americans at the three passes in the western three miles of the ridge, but had sent only five scouts to watch Jamaica Pass, three miles farther east. Behind the Heights of Guan, the country dipped, then rose again to Brooklyn Heights, where Major General Israel Putnam was camped with another thirty-two hundred American troops.

On the night of August 26, Howe led ten thousand troops quietly north through Jamaica Pass, capturing the five surprised sentries. First light found the two-mile-long column marching west toward Brooklyn Heights, undetected by the American troops on the ridge. On the south side of the ridge, the rest of Howe's army began a slow-moving attack on the American lines to distract attention until the main force had completed its deadly encirclement.

The plan worked to perfection. At 9:00 A.M., the main British force captured the village of Bedford to the rear of the ridge and fired two heavy guns to signal a general attack. Redcoats and Hessians swarmed up the ridge from the south. Heavily outnumbered, the Americans were forced from the crest into the onrushing bayonets of the main force sweeping in from the north. Between the two overwhelming forces, the American regiments shattered. The survivors fled through the woods, leaving behind hundreds of dead, wounded, and captured.

On the far western end of the ridge, Brigadier General William Alexander, an American officer known as Lord Stirling because of his claim to an ancient Scottish title, fought ferociously to cover the American retreat. Six times he led three Maryland

The American general Lord Stirling and his men sustained heavy casualties at the Battle of Long Island in August 1776.

companies in desperate charges before finally surrendering. Watching from Brooklyn Heights, Washington reportedly cried out, "Good God! What brave fellows I must this day lose!" In all, he lost just over a thousand, the British less than four hundred.

The Siege of Brooklyn Heights

The battle was over by 11:00 A.M., leaving Howe with the entire afternoon to launch an attack on Brooklyn Heights. Instead, he ordered his eager troops to camp and prepare to take the heights by siege. Inside the fortifications, the Americans waited, bruised and dispirited. The overwhelming British numbers and the lay of the land had made defeat inevitable. The Americans' poor planning, scouting, and coordination had turned defeat into disaster. Washington had trusted too much in his inexperienced commanders. Sullivan had neglected the crucial pass. Putnam had failed to order a withdrawal of the troops on the ridge when the British encirclement had been detected at the last minute.

Washington stubbornly refused to see the hopelessness of his position. Instead of ordering a retreat across the river, he called for reinforcements from Manhattan while a northeasterly wind kept British warships out of the river. For two days the armies dug and skirmished. A cold rain poured, dampening powder and making muskets unusable. At any time, Howe could have ordered an overwhelming bayonet charge, but instead he waited—the lion was proving sluggish.

The Retreat

On August 28, the truth about his situation finally dawned on Washington. He ordered all the boats that could be found in

Manhattan gathered by dark. He told all but his senior staff that he intended to bring reinforcements across. Instead he prepared a skillful retreat. Two regiments of Massachusetts fishermen brought the empty boats across the river after dark. All night long, troops crowded into the boats. Commands were whispered as men bundled the army's provisions and cannon aboard barges. Washington seemed to be everywhere, quietly giving orders and words of encouragement.

A skeleton force manned the fortifications through the early morning hours. At last, they too moved quietly to the boats. Suspicious of the silence, British scouts slipped into the camp. At first light, they pushed to the river, only to see the American rear guard rowing away. The last man to step into the last boat had been George Washington.

Manhattan

Washington had saved his army in one of the great feats of the war, but on reaching Manhattan, he again became indecisive. Not until September 12 did he order a retreat from the city. By then it was almost too late. The Americans were still loading their supplies when Howe struck at Kip's Bay north of the city on September 15. His troops scattered the raw militia guarding the shore. Washington and Putnam tried to stem the retreat. Washington became so enraged that he struck retreating soldiers with his riding crop, then stubbornly sat his horse in the face of the onrushing Hessians. An aide grabbed the horse's bridle and led Washington away.

Always best in a disaster, Putnam galloped south to the city, mustered the troops, and led them up the west side of Manhattan. The troops narrowly escaped the British trap. After an exhausting march, Putnam's men joined the rest of the army at Harlem Heights south of Kingsbridge and the Harlem River.

Howe camped two miles from the American lines. On the morning of September 16, American scouts and British light infantry collided. The scouts bloodied the light infantry, then withdrew. A British officer interpreted the withdrawal as another rout and ordered his bugler to sound the fox-hunting call. Watching from the heights, Washington heard the insulting notes. His face turned dark with anger. He ordered several regiments forward to teach the British a lesson. A sharp fight followed. The Americans fought European style—upright at close range—and thrashed some of the king's best troops.

The small victory pumped new spirit into the American army and made Howe even more cautious. Rather than attack the American lines in a frontal assault, he tried to get behind them by landing a force on the East River shore. Washington saw the encirclement coming and withdrew across the Harlem River to the mainland. On October 28, the armies faced each other at White Plains. Howe hit the American left with about five thousand men—a third of his force. The Americans fought doggedly, then retreated to a stronger position. History records the battle as a British victory, but its savagery convinced Howe to withdraw to the south.

Playing the Fox

The campaign was teaching Washington important lessons. His men had the stuff to be good soldiers, but only with training and experience. Congress had authorized a continental army, but most of his troops belonged to militia regiments raised by the individual colonies. Committed to serving only a few months, militiamen were dangerously inexperienced and unreliable. Even his continental troops had enlisted for only a year, barely enough time to get them trained. He must have men willing to soldier as long as there was fighting to be done. Congress had agreed to longer enlistments and more funds in October, but until the new regiments could be raised, Washington must preserve his army at all costs. He must play the fox, avoiding any battle that could risk the complete destruction of his army and the American cause.

As winter weather approached, Washington divided his shrinking forces. He stationed thirty-two hundred men under General William Heath at Peekskill to guard the invasion route to New England. General Charles Lee would keep fifty-five hundred more in the vicinity of White Plains to watch Howe. Washington would take the remaining three thousand into New Jersey to counter a British move toward Philadelphia. On November 10, Washington's troops crossed the Hudson and camped at Hackensack. Their general rode south with his staff on an important mission.

Disaster at Fort Washington

Early in the campaign, the Americans had built Fort Lee on the western shore of the Hudson and Fort Washington on the Manhattan side. The forts were supposed to prevent British warships from sailing up the river but had proved useless. Nathanael Greene, one of Washington's best generals, thought they should be held anyway. Against his better judgment, Washington had allowed Greene to maintain the forts while the main army retreated north toward White Plains. Now Washington intended to order Greene out of the forts.

Washington arrived too late and could only watch the worst disaster of the autumn unfold. On November 16, Howe threw eight thousand men against the outlying posts of Fort Washington. Driven into the fort, twenty-five hundred defenders huddled in an area barely big enough for a thousand. The fort's commander, Colonel Robert Magaw, saw that a cannonade would turn his fort into a slaughterhouse. He surrendered. In addition to the prisoners, the British captured 146 cannon, 12,000 artillery rounds, 2,800 muskets, 400,000 cartridges, and immense amounts of miscellaneous provisions. For Washington's ill-equipped army, the loss of supplies was a terrible blow.

Three days later, the British almost bagged Washington. Lord Charles Cornwallis, Howe's best field general, brought four thousand men across the Hudson in a night attack on Fort Lee. Alerted at the last minute, Washington, Greene, and the fort's garrison fled into the night.

Hide-and-Seek

For nearly three weeks, Washington and Cornwallis played a dangerous game of hide-and-seek. Washington led his ragged army south through New Jersey. Many of the men had no blankets, shoes, or shirts. They suffered terribly from cold, hunger, and fatigue. Behind them came the strong and well-equipped British. Several times Cornwallis nearly trapped the Americans, but Washington's skill, luck, and iron determination saved his army every time. On December 8, he led his men across the Delaware River, leaving no boats behind for the British.

Washington's exhausted army threw itself down on the Pennsylvania side of the river. Threadbare, cold, and hungry, men curled up by fires and slept like the dead. Their safety was fragile. The British would build boats or wait for the river to freeze and cross on the ice. In a few days, weeks at most, the pursuit would begin again. Washington looked at his small, ragged army and knew that little hope remained. "I think," he told a nephew, "the game is pretty near up."

★ 6 ★

The Darkest Hour

On the shores of the Delaware, the cause of American liberty faced its darkest hour. Only the river and Washington's ragged army stood between the British army and Philadelphia, a bare thirty miles to the south. Against the ten thousand British and Hessian regulars in New Jersey, Washington had an army of three thousand and a few companies of local militia. At the end of December the enlistments of most of the men would expire, leaving Washington with no more than fourteen hundred men.

Fear swept Philadelphia. Thousands fled the city with all the possessions they could carry. Loyalists hooted the departing and made ready to welcome generals Cornwallis and Howe. The Continental Congress hastily granted Washington power to continue the war without further instructions and moved to Baltimore on December 12.

The confident General Howe and his brother, Admiral Richard Howe, issued a proclamation offering pardons to all who would take an oath of loyalty to the king. Thousands flocked to the king's banner, including more than a few prominent soldiers and politicians.

"Times that Try Men's Souls"

Thomas Paine watched the unraveling of the American cause with rage and disgust. Since the publication of "Common Sense," he had been carrying a musket, but now he took up a weapon he understood far better, his pen. In mid-December, a press in Philadelphia began printing the first of fourteen pamphlets, which Paine entitled "The American Crisis." It opened: "These are the times that try men's souls: The summer soldier and the sunshine patriot will in this crisis, shrink from the service of his country; but he that stands it now, deserves the love and thanks of man and woman. Tyranny, like hell, is not easily conquered; yet we have this consolation with us, that the harder the conflict, the more glorious the triumph."

In days, copies of "The American Crisis" were circulating far beyond Philadelphia. In villages and on isolated farms, wavering patriots read the pamphlet and resolved to stand fast. Washington had his troops assembled to hear Paine's words. They returned to their cold posts determined to carry on as long as humanly possible.

The Ambitious General

Paine's words arrived about the same time the army received a terrible shock: news of the capture of Major General Charles Lee. Lee was Washington's second-in-command and the most respected professional soldier in the army. Washington himself stood a bit in awe of Lee, who had fought bravely in European wars. Lee despised Washington as an amateur. Many agreed and thought Lee, not Washington, should be leading the American army.

Left behind at White Plains to wait until Howe's plans became clear, Lee had ignored numerous requests from Washington to march south into New Jersey. He had finally crossed the Hudson on December 2, but lingered in northern New Jersey, unwilling to give up his independent command. On December 13, he camped his troops at Vealtown, then rode three miles to take comfortable lodgings at an inn. At dawn, a British cavalry patrol surrounded the inn and took Lee prisoner.

Washington and his troops were stunned by the news, but it was probably a blessing in disguise. Though a talented soldier, Lee was a proud and unreliable subordinate—one Washington could ill afford in the hour of crisis. Lee's second-in-command, General John Sullivan, marched Lee's two thousand troops promptly to Washington's aid.

Howe Surprises Everyone

Despite Paine's stirring pamphlet, the capture of Lee might have finished the Continental army's morale except for an extraordinary decision by General Howe. Instead of waiting for the arrival of boats or for the Delaware to freeze, Howe decided that he had done enough fighting for one year. On December 14, he ordered his troops into winter quarters in a long series of outposts from Trenton on the Delaware to Staten Island. The general returned to New York City for a season of parties and tributes to his military genius. General Cornwallis prepared to depart for leave in England.

Washington could hardly believe his luck. Immediately, he

started planning a desperate move to revive the American cause. He would cross the Delaware and risk his army against the Hessians at Trenton.

Night Crossing

The American army marched late on Christmas Day 1776. Two forces would cross south of Trenton, one to block a retreat by the Hessians, the other to delay reinforcements from farther south. Washington would lead the main force, some twenty-four hundred picked men with eighteen field guns, across the Delaware above Trenton, then march south to attack the town.

It was a terrible night. Wind, sleet, and snow lashed the men in the boats. Ice chunks filled the river, slowing the crossing and putting the plan hours behind schedule. The commanders of the two southern forces turned back, assuming that Washington would do the same. But Washington's iron will kept his troops moving. By 3:00 A.M., his men were ashore and marching south. Many of the soldiers wore only rags on their feet and left bloody footprints in the snow. The snow turned to rain, soaking the men and rendering their muskets useless except as clubs or handles for bayonets. Many of the officers were deeply discouraged, believing that the army was about to die in the final battle of a doomed cause. They were completely and gloriously wrong.

The Americans hit the northern Hessian outposts just before 8:00 A.M., driving the defenders into Trenton. Washington's regiments swept left and right to surround the town. The marvelously disciplined Hessian troops rushed from their quarters, formed, and charged up the two main streets. Grapeshot from the American field guns tore their ranks apart. The American

*George Washington and his forces crossing
the Delaware River on Christmas Day, 1776*

troops swarmed into Trenton. The Hessians regrouped at the southern edge of town and charged again. The Americans met them with field guns, bayonets, swords, and what muskets would still fire.

By 9:00 A.M., it was over. The Hessians had suffered 22 killed, 92 wounded, and 948 taken prisoner. Only four Americans had been wounded. Washington had originally planned to continue on to Princeton and New Brunswick, but the terrible night march had taken its toll. Unsupported by the two forces that should have landed to the south, he withdrew to the far side of the Delaware.

Princeton

Three days later, Washington led his army back across the river. At Assunpink Creek, just south of Trenton, his troops collided with the advance guard of a force led by Cornwallis, who had hastily returned from New York. In a fierce, late-afternoon fight, the Americans kept the British from crossing the creek. Cornwallis surveyed the situation and decided to delay another attack until morning, when he would have all of his fifty-five hundred men in position. An aide cautioned him that General Washington might not be waiting in the morning. Cornwallis laughed. He had the fox trapped and would "bag" him the next day.

Washington called his generals together. The army was outgunned, outnumbered, and without enough boats or time to retreat across the river. Once again, disaster seemed certain. Then someone proposed a bold plan: the army would slip around Cornwallis's left flank in the night and hit Princeton twelve miles to his rear. The army began preparing. A company was assigned to keep the campfires burning and to make the noise of furious digging. At 1:00 A.M., the rest of the army crept away, muskets unloaded, field gun wheels padded to soften the noise of their movement on the frozen road.

Sunrise on the chill, frosty morning of January 3, 1777, found the Americans closing on Princeton. Two of the three British regiments in town were already on the march to support Cornwallis. Outside the town, the British commander, Lieutenant Colonel Charles Mawhood, caught sight of two regiments of Americans. Both forces raced for the cover of an orchard. Forty yards apart they exchanged volleys. Mawhood led his troops in a charge. At the sight of the glittering rows of bayonets, the American regiments broke.

Then Washington galloped his horse through the retreating men. He was waving his hat, shouting for the men to rally. Only thirty yards from the British lines, he made a perfect target. A volley roared, hiding the general in a cloud of powder smoke. It drifted away, revealing Washington still astride his great white horse, still yelling for his men to take courage. Three more American regiments charged into the fight. The broken regiments re-formed and attacked.

Nearly surrounded, Mawhood's men fought like demons. American grapeshot ripped into their ranks. Mawhood led part of his force in a desperate charge that broke through the American lines. The Americans pursued, shooting down many and capturing fifty. The rest of the redcoats retreated from the orchard to Princeton. Some escaped through town, others surrendered. The fight had lasted only fifteen minutes, but Washington estimated British losses at one hundred killed and nearly three hundred captured. He had lost only forty killed or wounded.

The Escape

Cornwallis, staring angrily at the empty American lines at Trenton, heard the distant sound of cannon fire. He mustered his men and sent them hurrying toward Princeton. They arrived as the American rear guard was pulling out of the far end of town. Cornwallis guessed the Americans were headed for the British supply depot at New Brunswick. He hurried his troops down another road to get ahead of the Americans.

But Washington the Fox truly deserved his nickname now. He swung his army north and made for Morristown, a village on a protected plateau where winter quarters were already being prepared. On January 6, the weary but triumphant army straggled into Morristown.

The Cause Rekindled

The American cause had survived its darkest hour. Many more gloomy times lay ahead, but never again would the Revolution's future seem quite so desperate. The reputation of the army soared as news of the victories at Trenton and Princeton spread. Criticism of Washington changed to loud praise. Men reread "The American Crisis" and made ready to join the fight. General Howe pulled most of his forces out of New Jersey and brooded on the disgrace a few ragged rebels had heaped on his proud army.

In Europe, Benjamin Franklin and other American representatives pressed the French for aid. The French king and ministers were still unconvinced that the Americans could win, but they agreed to send military supplies in secret.

American and British troops continued to fight skirmishes throughout the winter. In New Jersey and New York, militiamen ambushed British and Loyalist troops foraging for supplies. At Morristown, Washington's army slowly recovered its strength. Sick and exhausted veterans went home, but new recruits trickled into camp. By late spring Washington had six thousand troops, with another three thousand scheduled to arrive soon. Ahead lay a long summer of careful maneuvering. His soldiers would not fight another pitched battle until fall. However, an American army in northern New York would have fighting aplenty.

★ 7 ★

—————— "Victory Writ Large" ——————

Lake Champlain had fascinated both sides since the early days of the war. The Americans had seen it as the route for an invasion of Canada. The British victory at Trois-Rivières in June 1776 had ended those dreams, and the lake had become the means for a mighty British invasion of the thirteen colonies.

In the summer of 1776, Canada's governor, General Sir Guy Carleton, built a fleet at St. John's to dominate the lake. He planned to capture Fort Ticonderoga, then follow Lake George to the Hudson River Valley. Once on the Hudson, he would take Albany, then march south to join Howe in the vicinity of New York. His advance would split the colonies. Cut off from New England, the Middle Atlantic and southern colonies—always less certain about the Revolution—might then make peace.

Valcour Island

Standing in Carleton's way were Major General Philip Schuyler and his brilliant subordinate, Benedict Arnold. Arnold built a small fleet of sailing ships and row galleys to oppose Carleton.

The two fleets met at Valcour Island on October 11, 1776. Outnumbered and outgunned, Arnold lost several ships and was forced to burn the rest. Yet Carleton had lost weeks of valuable summer weather preparing for the battle. He could not risk a fall siege of Fort Ticonderoga and a winter march on Albany. He withdrew to St. John's to wait for spring.

Carleton's second-in-command, Major General John Burgoyne, was disappointed. At fifty-four years old, Burgoyne felt that every delay reduced his chances for glory. He returned to England in the winter and presented Lord George Germain, the minister in charge of the war, with a plan for the summer campaign of 1777.

In addition to an advance south through Lake Champlain, Burgoyne suggested an invasion of New York's Mohawk Valley by way of Lake Ontario, the Oswego River, and Oneida Lake. The diversion would pull American defenders from the southern end of Lake Champlain. More important, it might swing the powerful Iroquois Indian tribes and the uncommitted colonists of the area to the British side. At Albany, the Mohawk Valley force would join the main invasion force from Lake Champlain for a triumphal march down the Hudson. Germain and King George approved the plan, naming Burgoyne commander of the main force. Burgoyne sailed for Canada with high hopes.

Almost immediately, Lord Germain began to have doubts. South of Lake Champlain, Burgoyne's supply lines would become dangerously long. Any delay on the march would give the Americans time to gather forces. If fall caught Burgoyne still above Albany, there might be a disaster. Germain wrote to General Howe, suggesting a move up the Hudson to join Burgoyne. Howe did not receive the letter until August 6, when he was already embarked on an invasion of Pennsylvania by way of Chesapeake Bay. Howe decided to continue with his plans,

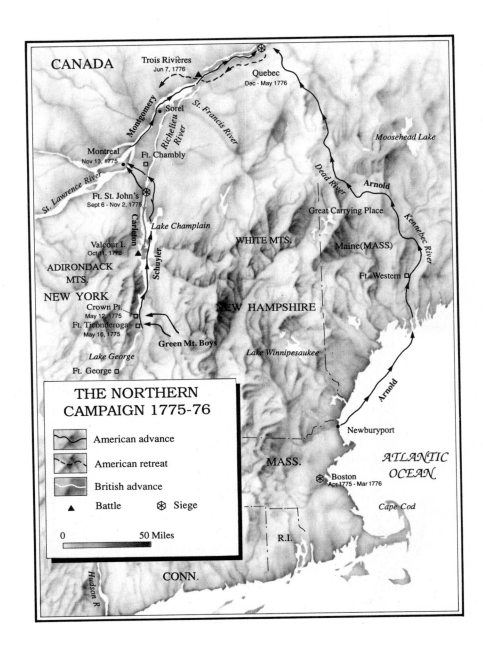

CANADA

Trois Rivières
Jun 7, 1776

Quebec
Dec - May 1776

Montgomery

Sorel

St. Francis River

Richelieu River

Montreal
Nov 13, 1775

Ft. Chambly

Moosehead Lake

St. Lawrence River

Ft. St. John's
Sept 6 - Nov 2, 1775

Carleton

Lake Champlain

Dead River

Arnold

Great Carrying Place

Kennebec River

WHITE MTS.

Maine(MASS.)

Valcour I.
Oct 11, 1776

Schuyler

ADIRONDACK
MTS.

Ft. Western

NEW YORK

NEW HAMPSHIRE

Crown Pt.
May 12, 1775

Ft. Ticonderoga
May 10, 1775

Green Mt. Boys

Lake George

Ft. George

Lake Winnipesaukee

Arnold

Newburyport

*ATLANTIC
OCEAN*

MASS.

Boston
Apr 1775 - Mar 1776

Cape Cod

R.I.

Hudson R.

CONN.

THE NORTHERN
CAMPAIGN 1775-76

American advance

American retreat

British advance

▲ Battle   ⊛ Siege

0   50 Miles

instructing General Henry Clinton, commander of the garrison at New York, to cooperate with Burgoyne if circumstances permitted.

Gentleman Johnny

At St. John's, Burgoyne assembled a force of 8,300 men, including over 3,000 Hessians, 650 Loyalists and Canadians, and some 400 Indians. He sent a proclamation south promising "devastation, famine and . . . horror" to those who opposed the king. The proclamation was a mistake. Its insulting tone and its threat of unleashing thousands of Indians in a "phrenzy of hostility" so angered the Americans that they took up arms by the thousands.

Burgoyne had few doubts that he could back his words with action. John Burgoyne thought well of himself. A handsome, rather fleshy man, he was famed in London society as a wit, a playwright, and a member of Parliament. In most respects, he was an able general, well liked by his troops, who called him Gentleman Johnny. Yet Burgoyne lacked the ability of Howe or the drive of Cornwallis. He misunderstood the difficulties of campaigning in the wilderness. Summers were short in the North, and he would have to move fast through rough and hostile country. His army was ill equipped for the task. His men wore tight, heavy European uniforms. Without horses, his German cavalry clumped along in thigh-high boots weighing twelve pounds. The army had too few oxen for its long train of artillery, but it carried far too many luxuries, including Burgoyne's mistress and servants.

On the Move

The expedition got off to a good start, reaching Fort Ticonderoga by water on July 1, 1777. After a brief siege, the American commander, Brigadier General Arthur St. Clair, abandoned the fort under cover of darkness. He sent his supplies south on the lake, then led the garrison overland. Burgoyne sent his dashing and able subordinate, Brigadier General Simon Fraser, after St. Clair. At dawn on July 7, Fraser's light infantry caught the American rear guard at Hubbardton. A sharp fight left four hundred Americans dead, wounded, and captured, but at the cost of two hundred British casualties—troops that Burgoyne could ill afford to lose.

Burgoyne and the main force sailed south after St. Clair's fleeing supply boats. At Skenesboro on the southern end of the lake, the Americans burned most of their boats and supplies and escaped into the woods.

The Wrong Road

The easy part of the campaign was over. Burgoyne hesitated. In front of him lay twenty-three miles of wilderness road through deep forest to Fort Edward on the Hudson. A better route lay to the west, across the portage between Lake Champlain and Lake George, then over a good ten-mile road to Fort Edward. Yet the better route involved a short detour to the north, and Burgoyne refused to take even that small step backward. He would send his artillery and most of the supplies by the water route, but his army must march forward. It was a terrible decision.

General Schuyler sent a thousand axmen into the woods to delay Burgoyne, while the American army gathered at Albany. The woodsmen destroyed forty bridges, chopped down huge trees to block the road, and diverted streams to create swamps. British engineers repaired the damage, but three precious weeks slipped by before Burgoyne reached the abandoned Fort Edward on July 29.

With supplies running low, Burgoyne dispatched the German Lieutenant Colonel Friedrich Baum and 700 men, including the footsore cavalry, on a raid to gather cattle, horses, and whatever else they could find. On August 16, Brigadier General John Stark of Bunker Hill fame pounced on Baum's force near Bennington, Vermont, and virtually wiped it out. A support column of 650 more Germans arrived on the battlefield just in time to receive much the same treatment. In all, Burgoyne's army lost over 900 of its best troops, killed or captured, while Stark's militia suffered only 30 killed and 40 wounded. The summer was turning gloomy for Gentleman Johnny, and it was about to get worse.

Fort Stanwix and Oriskany

In July, Lieutenant Colonel Barry St. Leger had begun the western invasion of New York by way of Lake Ontario with about 1,750 men, more than half of them unreliable Indian recruits. Fort Stanwix at the head of the Mohawk River lay in his way, garrisoned by a small but tough force of continentals under Colonel Peter Gansevoort. St. Leger laid siege to the fort, then sent most of his Indians and Loyalists to meet a strong force of militia marching to the fort's aid. They surrounded the militia near Oriskany on August 6, but the Americans formed a circle to beat back the attack. After heavy losses, both sides retreated.

While the fight at Oriskany raged, Gansevoort sent his men into the lightly defended British camp. They overpowered the guards and gleefully burned all the supplies they could not carry back to the fort.

St. Leger surveyed the burned remains of his camp. With his supplies gone, his Indian allies deserting, and another strong American force approaching—this time under the feared Benedict Arnold—St. Leger had little choice left. He abandoned the expedition. Burgoyne received news of the disaster in late August; he would get no help from the west.

Blocking the Way

Burgoyne's army plodded south. Already, Burgoyne had lost over two thousand men in battle or to the hardships of the march. On September 13, he crossed the Hudson to get on the Albany side of the river. Not far south, the rapidly growing American army lay in wait under its new commander, General Horatio Gates. Gates had done a masterful job of finding troops. He had published stories of outrages committed by Burgoyne's Indians, then watched with satisfaction as new recruits streamed into camp. He put them to work digging earthworks along Bemis Heights, north of the juncture of the Mohawk and Hudson rivers. On September 17, scouts brought word that Burgoyne's army had arrived.

Separated by four miles of heavy woods, neither side had a good idea of the other's positions. Gates held his seven thousand men behind the fortifications and waited for an attack. Benedict Arnold saw the danger in letting Burgoyne choose the time and place for battle. He argued for an attack, but Gates refused. Gates was a political general, adept at dealing with Congress and managing the Continental army's paperwork, but he was not an experienced or talented field commander. Worse, he did not recognize his weaknesses.

Freeman's Farm

On September 19, Burgoyne launched his assault. His left wing under the German general, Baron von Riedesel, would guard the army's supplies and the riverbank. Burgoyne would attack the American center, holding Gates's attention while Fraser led his light infantry around the American left to seize an undefended hill beyond the American lines. With cannon on the high ground, Fraser would drive the rebels from their fortifications. The whole British army would then advance to destroy the American forces piecemeal.

The deadly intent of Fraser's flanking movement was soon obvious to Arnold, and he almost went mad trying to get permission for a counterattack. Finally, Gates agreed to send Colonel Daniel Morgan to head off the flanking movement. Morgan was an extraordinary figure, a veteran of Arnold's march on Quebec and numerous other adventures. His riflemen were among the best fighters in the army. In a sharp fight, they stopped Fraser's light infantry.

Arnold saw his chance. Without permission, he hurled his troops against Burgoyne's center as the British troops advanced into a clearing known as Freeman's Farm. Only 350 yards long, the clearing became the site of perhaps the most savage battle of the Revolution. Morgan and Arnold led their troops in charge after charge to drive the British back from their cannon. Burgoyne and Brigadier General James Hamilton led men just as brave in counterattacks. Bodies piled around the guns. The British 62nd Regiment almost ceased to exist, as 290 of its 350 men fell. The British fire began to weaken. With only one or two more regiments, Arnold could break the British center, cutting Burgoyne's army in two for Gates to destroy. Gates did nothing. Baron von Riedesel did. Leaving the supplies practically unguarded, he hurried to Burgoyne's aid. His fresh troops forced the exhausted Americans from the field.

Arnold was furious. He had bloodied the British, inflicting some six hundred casualties while losing about half that number, but the great chance had been missed. When he learned that Gates's report on the battle did not even mention his name, Arnold exploded. Gates promptly removed him from command. Only the begging of his fellow officers kept Arnold from going home.

Burgoyne Waits for Help

Burgoyne planned to attack again the next day, but delayed on receiving a letter from General Clinton in New York City. Fearing that the messenger might be captured, Clinton had kept the letter brief. Dated September 11, it stated that Clinton would "push at Montgomery in about ten days." "Montgomery" referred to an American fort forty miles up the Hudson from New York. Burgoyne was overjoyed, believing that a major expedition was coming north to meet him. He dug in to wait for Clinton. Unaware of the danger Burgoyne was in, Clinton had no intention of creating more than a diversion to draw American troops from upper New York. He captured forts Montgomery and Clinton on October 6, but by then nothing could save Gentleman Johnny from his fate.

Victory at Bemis Heights

Burgoyne's wait for Clinton proved fatal. By October 7, Gates had eleven thousand men, nearly twice the British number. Burgoyne's generals argued for an immediate retreat, but Burgoyne decided on one last attempt to break through to Albany. He would send out a large scouting party to test the American left wing. Perhaps the high ground Fraser had tried to reach on the day of Freeman's Farm could still be taken.

About twelve hundred picked troops moved out from Burgoyne's fortifications on the morning of October 7. In a wheat field they spread out in a long line, then waited as their generals studied the woods ahead and foragers cut hay for the army's remaining horses. Informed of the strangely immobile line in the wheat field, Gates decided to risk an attack. Hidden by the woods, two American columns moved quietly to flank the British left and right. At 2:30 P.M. they poured out of the woods in such force that the British left and right crumpled. Only the German troops in the center held.

In the American camp, Benedict Arnold leaped on his horse and, ignoring the shouts of Gates's aide, spurred into the battle. No one on the field questioned his right to command, as he shouted orders to the regimental officers. On the other side, General Fraser desperately rallied his men. Arnold yelled to Morgan, "That man on the gray horse . . . must be disposed of." One of Morgan's riflemen climbed a tree and shot down the daring Fraser. The remaining British and Germans gave way.

Arnold led the Americans on the left in a mad pursuit. They assaulted a redoubt and were thrown back. Arnold wheeled his horse and dashed across the line of fire to redirect the American right. The troops burst through a soft point in the British fortifications. Arnold fell wounded, and the American attack gradually lost momentum. But at dusk the Americans held the center of the British fortifications with Burgoyne's remaining positions at their mercy.

Surrender at Saratoga

That night, Burgoyne began his retreat. Cut off from escape across the Hudson, he took defensive positions on the heights of Saratoga a few miles from the battleground. The glorious army that had set forth in June now lay shivering and hungry in the autumn rain. Night after night American cannon lobbed

shells into the camp, and rebel snipers crept close to pick off sentries. Hope gone, Burgoyne agreed to surrender his fifty-eight hundred remaining troops.

The destruction of Burgoyne's army marked the beginning of a new day for the cause of liberty. France would enter the war soon after the news reached Paris. Its army and navy would prove decisive in winning the war. Even more important, the great victory gave the citizens of the embattled colonies new hope. Many Americans—even those of firm patriotic faith—had never quite believed that the Revolution could be won. But at Saratoga, they saw the might of the British Empire brought low— and believed.

Citizen Soldiers

On October 17, 1777, the British and German troops marched out of their camp on the heights of Saratoga to lay down their arms. They passed between long, silent ranks of American soldiers. One of the German veterans later wrote: "Not one of them was properly uniformed, but each man had on the clothes in which he goes to the field, to church or to the tavern. But they stood like soldiers."

The German veteran had never seen their like on the battlefields of Europe. These were citizen soldiers who fought not for the spoils of war but for the glory of a cause. They had carried on through defeats that would have crushed armies of

The British general John Burgoyne surrenders to General Horatio Gates at Saratoga on October 17, 1777.

professionals. And they would know defeat again, but the citizen soldiers and their families would survive the desperate times to come, as they had won through the dark hours of the early years. In the end, the American Revolution would not be a generals' victory, but the triumph of a people determined to live free.

Suggested Reading

Cook, Fred J. *Dawn over Saratoga.* New York: Doubleday, 1973.

Ketchum, Richard M., ed. *The Revolution.* New York: American Heritage, 1958.

Lengyel, Cornel. *The Declaration of Independence.* New York: Grosset and Dunlap, 1968.

McDowell, Bart. *The Revolutionary War.* Washington: National Geographic Society, 1967.

McPhillips, Martin. *The Battle of Trenton.* Morristown, New Jersey: Silver Burdett, 1985.

Middlekauff, Robert. *The Glorious Cause.* New York: Oxford University Press, 1982.

Sanderlin, George. *1776: Journals of American Independence.* New York: Harper & Row, 1968.

Ward, Christopher. *The War of the Revolution.* New York: Mac-·millan, 1952.

Wright, Esmond. *The Fire of Liberty.* New York: St. Martin's, 1983.

About the Author

Alden R. Carter is a versatile writer for children and young adults. He has written nonfiction books on electronics, supercomputers, radio, Illinois, and the People's Republic of China. His novels *Growing Season* (1984) and *Wart, Son of Toad* (1985) were named to the American Library Association's annual list of best books for young adults. His most recent novel is *Sheila's Dying*. His other books on the American Revolution are: *Colonies in Revolt, At the Forge of Liberty,* and *Birth of the Republic.* Mr. Carter lives with his wife, Carol, and their son, Brian Patrick, and daughter, Siri Morgan, in Marshfield, Wisconsin.